TRUE

STORIES

from the

TITANIC

SALLY SAMS

Published by Yellow Tulip Press
P.O.Box 211
Ben Lomond, CA 95005

Printed in U.S.A.

FOR
ED

FIRST SAILING OF THE LATEST ADDITION TO THE WHITE STAR FLEET

The Queen of the Ocean

TITANIC

LENGTH 882 FT.   OVER 45,000 TONS   BEAM 92 FT.
TRIPLE-SCREWS

This, the Latest, Largest and Finest Steamer Afloat, will sail from

WHITE STAR LINE, PIER 59 (North River), NEW YORK

Saturday, April 20th
At 12 Noon

All passengers berthed in closed rooms containing 2, 4, or 6 berths, a large number equipped with washstands, etc.

Spacious Dining Saloons
Smoking Room
Ladies' Reading Room
Covered Promenade

Reservations of Berths may be made direct with this Office or through any of our accredited Agents

THIRD CLASS RATES ARE:

To PLYMOUTH, SOUTHAMPTON, LONDON, LIVERPOOL and GLASGOW.	$36.25
To GOTHENBURG, MALMÖ, CHRISTIANIA, COPENHAGEN, ESBJERG, Etc.	41.50
To STOCKHOLM, ÅBO, HANGO, HELSINGFORS,	44.50
To HAMBURG, BREMEN, ANTWERP, AMSTERDAM, ROTTERDAM, HAVRE, CHERBOURG	45.00

TURIN, $48.   NAPLES, $51.50.   PIRAEUS, $55.   BEYROUTH, $61., Etc., Etc.

DO NOT DELAY.   Secure your tickets through the local Agents or direct from

WHITE STAR LINE, 9 Broadway, New York

TICKETS FOR SALE HERE

FOREWORD

The Age of Innocence. The Gilded Age. *La Belle Epoque.* No matter what you call it, the period that began in the last quarter of the nineteenth century and continued through the first decade of the twentieth was a time of unprecedented peace, prosperity and progress. It ended officially in the early morning hours of April 15, 1912, as the largest moving object ever made by man, the Royal Mail Steamer *Titanic,* finished her maiden voyage at the bottom of the Atlantic Ocean—taking with her more than 1,500 souls and the confidence of a generation.

The *Titanic* was a perfect reflection of the world of unbridled optimism into which she was born. Starting in the 1870s, there had been a dizzying array of new and profoundly exciting inventions: the electric light bulb, the telephone, sound recording, the automobile, the airplane, the motion picture camera. Life was so good, in fact, that the U.S. Patent Office briefly considered putting itself out of business, reasoning that everything had already been invented. There was simply no problem technology could not solve, no natural obstacle mankind's own inventiveness could not overcome.

The world of the *Titanic* was also one in which the line dividing the haves and the have-nots was perfectly drawn. There was no income tax on the new industrial-age millionaires—so the rich were incredibly, almost unfathomably rich. At the other end of the economic spectrum, there was no Social Security—and nothing to keep those on the bottom of the ladder from falling off entirely. Plus, wave after wave of new immigrants poured into the U.S., penniless but eager to begin a new life in the land of opportunity.

The *Titanic,* built in 1911 by Britain's White Star Line, represented both the best and worst in this age of prosperity and progress. Almost four city blocks long, she was not the fastest ship on the ocean—nor was she meant to be. The *Titanic* was built for safety and comfort, equipped with both the most advanced technology and the most luxurious appointments of any ship afloat.

Most striking to nautical experts was her watertight construction, based on a double bottom and a system of 16 separate watertight compartments formed by bulkheads that ran the entire length of the ship. The *Titanic* could stay afloat with any two of the compartments flooded—leading *Shipbuilding* magazine to devote a special issue to this new engineering marvel, pronouncing it "virtually unsinkable." The *Titanic* did have 20 lifeboats, but these were strictly a formality—more for public relations than to satisfy any real need. No one seemed troubled that there was room on the lifeboats for less than half the "unsinkable" ship's passengers.

Most impressive to the White Star Line's customers were the *Titanic's* glamorous amenities, including the First-Class Dining Salon, which rivaled the finest restaurants, a French-style sidewalk cafe, a state-of-the-art gymnasium, and private promenade decks off the luxurious First-Class suites.

The Grand Staircase

But for all its luxury, the *Titanic* was not built just for the *creme de la creme* of society. The White Star Line also planned to make money with Second-Class family trade and Third-Class immigrant passengers. The Third-Class accommodations, located below decks, were a completely different world from the posh First-Class suites above—and the two worlds rarely met.

The *Titanic's* maiden voyage was to be *the* event of the year. The rich and powerful from both sides of the Atlantic rushed to make reservations: Mr. and Mrs. John Jacob Astor IV, Benjamin Guggenheim, Lord and Lady Duff-Gordon, Mr. and Mrs. Isidor Straus. The president of the White Star Line, Bruce Ismay, was on board. So was Thomas Andrews, managing director of Harland and Wolff Ship-yard, the *Titanic's* builder. Even financier J.P. Morgan, whose company owned the White Star Line, was slated to make the trip—although he had to cancel at the last minute. In fact, so many luminaries were clamoring for First-Class passage on the *Titanic's* maiden voyage that some had to settle for Second Class instead.

Departing on April 10, 1912, the *Titanic* was to go from Southampton, England, to New York City with 2,207 passengers aboard. There were actresses and account-ants, industrialists and immigrants. And all the *Titanic's* passengers, from John Jacob Astor IV of First Class—on his way home after an extended European tour—to Assyrian immigrant and Third-Class passenger Philip Zenni—on his way to a new life in Cincinnati—were delighted to be traveling to New York on the most splendid ship ever built.

Then the unthinkable happened. Four days into the voyage, the "unsinkable" ship struck an iceberg that ripped holes in her skin for 300 feet and flooded the first six watertight compartments. Captain Edward Smith, White Star's most experienced and highly regarded captain, quickly dispatched crew members to assess the damage. He also called on the ship's builder, Thomas Andrews, who delivered the devastating news: The *Titanic* was going down.

Stewards began waking the First-Class passengers, helping them into their lifebelts and guiding them up to the deck. Crew members made announcements in Second and Third Class. Meanwhile, the ship's stokers, firemen, stewards, cooks, carpenters—even the musicians—stayed at their posts, working until the very end to keep the ship afloat with her lights burning.

For the First-Class passengers, it was a quick, cold ending to their smug and safe world. Some seemed more perturbed than frightened, like John Jacob Astor, who refused to get off the ship until it was too late. And Lady Duff-Gordon, who bemoaned the loss of her secretary's "beautiful nightdress" over the screams of the dying. Others, like pacifist and spiritualist William T. Stead, remained peaceful to the end. For actress Dorothy Gibson it was an adventure. Margaret "Molly" Brown fought all the way. Still others, like Benjamin Guggenheim and Mr. and Mrs. Isidor Straus, accepted their fate on their own terms. Some survived, some didn't. But they all went down in history together. These are their stories.

APRIL 14, 1912, 11 P.M.

The Titanic *receives a warning message from a nearby ship, the* Californian, *which has been stopped since 10:30, blocked by ice. Wireless operator Jack Phillips, busy with an overflowing basket of passengers' personal messages to send at the end of a long day, shoots back an impatient reply: "Shut up; shut up! I am busy...."*

THE UNSINKABLE MRS. BROWN

Margaret Tobin "Molly" Brown

I t was a long voyage for Margaret Tobin "Molly" Brown from a dirt-poor childhood to a luxurious First-Class cabin on the *Titanic*. But the ship's survivors were glad she made that voyage. Because when death looked Molly Brown in the eye, Molly Brown looked right back.

Today the public knows Mrs. Brown as "Molly," but that nickname comes from the 1960s musical comedy based on her life. In her own time, Mrs. Brown was known as Maggie.

How did Maggie Brown get from Hannibal, Missouri, to the *Titanic* and, eventually, to the Broadway stage and the movie screen? The story began in 1867, when Margaret Tobin was born to a ditch digger and his wife. With little formal education, she went to work in her early teens. At about the age of 17—inspired, she later said, by fellow Hannibal native Mark Twain—Maggie followed her brother west to the mining town of

Leadville, Colorado, where she found a job as a seamstress at the Daniel and Fisher department store. At a church picnic young Maggie met James Joseph "J.J." Brown, a native Pennsylvanian 13 years her senior who had also made his way west and was managing the Ibex Mining Company. Maggie and J.J. married in 1886.

Eight years later, in 1894, life changed forever when J.J. Brown struck gold in the Little Johnnie mine and became a millionaire. The Browns soon moved to Denver, where Maggie tried, at first unsuccessfully, to take her place in high society. There were obstacles in her way. Maggie Brown was Irish Catholic and *nouveau riche*—and considered gauche and garish by Denver's upper crust. Even so, Maggie's winning personality and J.J.'s fortune were ultimately too much to resist, and the Brown home eventually became the center of Denver society.

By all accounts, the Browns' marriage was never really a happy one, although it did produce two children, Lawrence and Catherine Ellen. Herself a child of poverty, Maggie had a big heart when it came to helping others. Sometimes her husband found that heart *too* big. When Maggie allowed a group of impoverished Indians to set up their tents on her front lawn after they had been driven off the grounds of the State Capitol, it was the last straw for J.J. He moved out.

Even though the marriage was for all purposes finished, J.J. continued to support his wife until his death. Maggie kept busy with her extravagant lifestyle, traveling to exotic ports around the world and mingling with the cream of society at home. She spent time in New York, Newport and Europe, becoming the life of the party among the Astors, Vanderbilts, Whitneys and other social leaders of the day. Although she enjoyed the high life, Brown continued to lavish just as much time and money on causes ranging from women's suffrage to Catholic charities.

In the spring of 1912, at age 44, Brown had just wintered in Egypt with the Astors after a luxurious ocean voyage on the *Olympic,* stopping off in Paris to visit her daughter, who was in finishing school there. The Astors encouraged Brown to book First-Class return passage with them on the maiden voyage of the impressive new *Titanic,* sister ship to the *Olympic.* Along with the Astors, Molly boarded the *Titanic* on April 10 when it stopped in Cherbourg, France.

When disaster struck the *Titanic* on the evening of April 14, Brown—unlike many of the more sheltered First-Class women on board—was able to keep her head about her. As a First-Class passenger and a woman, she was quickly whisked into lifeboat No. 6, under the command of Quartermaster Robert Hitchens. Brown helped row the boat and coaxed the other women to sing so that they could stop crying. After the *Titanic* sunk, she insisted on going back to try to rescue survivors who were still alive in the water. Hitchens refused, fearing desperate masses might swamp the small lifeboat and tip it over. At one point, Brown reportedly threatened to throw Hitchens overboard. Later, when they had been picked up by the the rescue ship *Carpathia,* Brown spent long hours nursing ill survivors who were not as fortunate as she had been.

When the ordeal of the *Titanic's* sinking was finally over, Brown, with her usual good humor, proclaimed: "Typical Brown luck, we're unsinkable." A legend was born as the American press picked up the phrase and celebrated Maggie as the "Unsinkable Mrs. Brown."

After filing an insurance claim against the White Star Line citing more than $27,000 in losses, Brown directed her charitable efforts toward helping the *Titanic's* survivors and their dependents. She raised more than $10,000 for the cause and also campaigned for maritime reform.

Her good works continued. During World War I, Brown, along with Sarah Bernhardt, received the French Legion of Honor for her contributions to the cause.

But after her husband's death in 1922, Brown saw her fortune—and her lifestyle—slowly ebb away. Her Denver mansion became a boarding house and Brown moved into the Brown Palace Hotel. She died in 1932, alone and in poverty, at New York's Barbizon-Club Hotel.

Even in death, Brown was unsinkable. In 1960 the story of Margaret Tobin Brown made it all the way to Broadway when Meredith Willson (*The Music Man*) wrote *The Unsinkable Molly Brown*, a heavily fictionalized musical version of Brown's story. The show was a hit and went on to become a 1964 film starring Debbie Reynolds. Molly Brown is also a pivotal character in James Cameron's wildly popular 1997 film *Titanic*, played by Oscar-winning actress Kathy Bates.

The Brown House in Denver

Molly Brown's home in Denver eventually fell into ruin, but in 1970 it was acquired and restored by Historic Denver. Today, the late Victorian mansion is a tourist attraction. And the Unsinkable Mrs. Brown is the stuff of legends.

April 14, 1912, 11:39 p.m.

Lookout Frederick Fleet is without binoculars—somehow, the set in the crow's nest has disappeared. Even so, near the end of his watch, he spots something in the dark water before him. As the ship draws closer, the object grows larger until Fleet knows exactly what it is. He rings the bell three times to signal danger as he gasps into the phone to the bridge, "Iceberg right ahead!"

THE RICHEST MAN
IN THE WORLD

Colonel and Mrs. John Jacob Astor IV

Although born into almost unimaginable wealth and privilege, Colonel John Jacob Astor IV had many accomplishments of his own—accomplishments that would all come to an end in the frigid North Atlantic in the early morning hours of April 15, 1912.

Born on July 13, 1864, in Rhinebeck, New York, Astor was the son of William Astor and great-grandson of wealthy fur trader and family founder John Jacob Astor. Young John grew up with every advantage money could buy, including an education at St. Paul's School and Harvard University.

After college Astor spent several years traveling through Europe until in 1891, at age 27, he finally settled back in New York to manage the family fortune. On May 1 of that year Astor married Ava Willing of Philadelphia and the two settled comfortably into homes on Fifth Avenue and at Ferncliff, Rhinebeck, New York.

But comfort was not enough for John Jacob Astor IV. Besides managing the family fortune, the forward-thinking Astor became a writer and prolific inventor. In 1894 Astor wrote a science fiction novel, *A Journey to Other Worlds.* He also invented, or helped to invent, several widely-used mechanical devices including the turbine engine, a pneumatic road-improver and a bicycle brake.

Astor was also involved in real estate on a grand scale. In 1897 he built the Astoria Hotel in New York, adjoining the Waldorf Hotel which had been built by his cousin William Waldorf Astor. The new complex became known as the Waldorf-Astoria. Astor later built two other hotels, the Hotel St. Regis in 1905 and the Knickerbocker in 1906.

The Waldorf-Astoria Hotel

Astor was also active in the military, becoming staff colonel to General Levi P. Morton. When the Spanish-American War broke out in 1898, Astor was commissioned as a lieutenant colonel in the U.S. volunteers. He placed his yacht at the disposal of the U.S. government and supplied artillery for use against the Spanish.

In 1909 Astor divorced Ava, with whom he had a son and a daughter. Two years later, at age 47 and amid much gossip, he married 18-year-old Madeleine Talmadge Force, who was a year younger than his son. Astor's marriage was considered not entirely respectable among many of his peers in the social elite. The newlyweds decided to handle the controversy by leaving it behind, spending much of the next three years abroad.

In 1912 Mr. and Mrs. Astor wintered in Egypt and Paris, spending time with friends including Margaret "Molly" Brown. Mrs. Astor was expecting their first child, so in the spring the Astors decided to return to America so the baby could be born at home. They booked First-Class passage on the splendid new *Titanic*, boarding when it docked in Cherbourg.

The Astors were awakened shortly after 11:40 p.m. on April 14 by a jolt. Mrs. Astor thought perhaps it was some mishap in the kitchen. Colonel Astor left his suite to investigate and returned a few minutes later to tell Madeleine that the ship had struck ice, but reassuring her that the damage did not seem serious.

Still, there was to be no more sleep for the Astors that night. Within half an hour both Astors were up on the boat deck where the First-Class passengers were gathered. Mrs. Astor looked as stylish as always in a fashionable light-colored dress. To escape the cold, the Astors ducked into the ship's gymnasium, sitting on the mechanical horses. The mood was still relatively light. Although the Astors put on their lifebelts, Colonel Astor, with his inventor's curiosity, found an extra belt and cut up the lining with his pocket knife to show his wife what the inside was made of.

With the hubris of one so privileged he cannot even imagine real disaster, Colonel Astor remained almost unnaturally calm—even as the passengers began filing onto the lifeboats. He was convinced that evacuating the ship was a precaution rather than a necessity. Astor even ridiculed the idea of trading the massive decks of the *Titanic* for a small lifeboat in the cold, choppy waters: "We are safer here than in that little boat."

By 1:45 a.m., Colonel Astor had reconsidered. As he helped his wife climb onto the lifeboat, Astor asked if he might be able to join her—especially seeing that she was in a "delicate" condition. No, the ship's officer told him, men would not be allowed to board the lifeboat until all the women had been seated.

Astor stood alone as his wife's boat sailed out into the cold Atlantic waters. His crushed body was recovered on Monday, April 22, by a passing ship and identified by the letters J.J.A. on the collar of his shirt.

Colonel Astor left Madeleine the income from a $5 million trust fund and the use of the two homes as long as she did not marry. In August 1912 Madeleine gave birth to a son whom she named John Jacob Astor V.

Eventually, Madeleine gave up the Astor income and mansions. During World War I she married William K. Dick of New York and later had two more sons. She divorced Dick in Reno in 1933 to marry Italian prize fighter Enzo Firemonte. Five years later this marriage also ended in divorce. Madeleine died in Palm Beach, Florida, in 1940 at the age of 47.

APRIL 14, 1912, 11:40 P.M.

T he bow of the ship swings to port, but not quickly enough. The Titanic scrapes an enormous iceberg, creating a series of holes in the ship's steel skin. Shards of ice fly onto the deck and a shudder goes through the bowels of the ship. Passengers—many of them jarred out of a sound sleep—begin to speculate on what happened. The Titanic lies dead in the water.

THE SPIRITUALIST WHO PREDICTED DISASTER

William Thomas Stead

By the time he boarded the *Titanic* at the age of 62, Englishman William Thomas Stead—editor, spiritualist, peace crusader and rugged individualist—had seen and done more than most men of his age or any age. But had he foreseen his own fate?

In 1886, Stead had published an article with eerie parallels to the *Titanic* disaster. "How the Mail Steamer Went Down in Mid-Atlantic, By a Survivor" was the tale of an unnamed steamship equipped with too few lifeboats. The steamer collides with another ship—and, like the *Titanic*, loses many lives. Stead annotated the article with an editorial comment, warning that this scenario could easily happen again in real life if ships were not properly equipped with lifeboats.

Was the article a premonition of the *Titanic* disaster? Stead enthusiasti-

cally promoted spiritualism in all its many forms, including channeling

and spirit photography, and was a staunch supporter of various spiri-

tual mediums. Throughout his life he had premonitions, many of them

involving disasters at sea.

Traveling on the *Titanic* in his capacity as a pacifist, Stead was making the

voyage at the behest of President William Howard Taft. He was headed to

New York to participate in a world peace conference at Carnegie Hall on

April 21. Before boarding the doomed ocean liner, Stead had a premonition

that something good would result from the voyage. Perhaps, in a strange

way, for Stead the outcome of his voyage on the *Titanic* was good.

When he boarded the *Titanic,* Stead had homes in both London and Hayling

Island, Hampshire. But he was born in Northumbria on July 5, 1849, the son

of Reverend W. Stead, a minister, and Isabella Jobson Stead, daughter of a

Yorkshire farmer. The family soon moved to Howden-on-Tyne, where Stead

was schooled by his father until age 12. In 1861 Stead went to Silcoates School

near Wakefield. In 1863, at age 14, his formal education ended and Stead was

apprenticed as an office boy in a merchant's counting house.

The lack of an advanced education proved no barrier to the bright young

man. By the age of 21, Stead's love of writing led him to begin contributing

articles to the *Northern Echo,* a new liberal paper being published in Darling-
ton. During this time, Stead had his first premonition, that he had the favor of
the paper's senior partner. Within a year the premonition proved true as
Stead became editor of the fledgling publication. In 1873 Stead married
Emma Lucy Wilson, with whom he went on to have six children.

On January 1, 1880, Stead had a premonition that he would soon be working
in London. By February he had accepted a position as assistant editor of London's *Pall Mall Gazette,* another liberal publication. A few years later Stead
took over as editor, developing the paper into a vocal supporter of political
and social movements.

In 1885 Stead stirred up controversy by publishing an expose' on child prosti-
tution and white slavery that led to the government raising the age of consent
to 16. In his article, Stead reported purchasing a 13-year-old girl and taking
her to Paris. The public was outraged and Stead was denounced as obscene
from pulpits all over England. Since Stead had never gotten a receipt for purchasing the girl, he could not prove his allegations. He was tried for abduct-
ing her and wound up spending three months in jail.

Eventually Stead tired of the daily grind of the *Pall Mall Gazette* and went on
to found several other publications, including the *Review of Reviews,* the *American Review of Reviews* and the *Australian Review of Reviews.* He also founded
the Masterpiece Library of Penny Poets, Novels and Prose Classics.

Around 1890 Stead's dalliance with the supernatural became a passion. His guide through the world of the spirits was Julia Ames, editor of a Chicago publication called *The Woman's Union Signal,* who had died a year after their meeting but whom he had embraced as a kindred spirit.

By 1892 Stead had discovered the ability to write automatically and penned many letters he claimed were channeled through the spirits of others, including Empress Catherine the Great and the late prime minister Gladstone. The most frequent user of his hand, he claimed, was Julia Ames. From 1893 to 1897, Stead edited *Borderland,* a periodical devoted to spiritualism that included a column called "Letters From Julia."

Stead believed Julia was encouraging him to start an organization to help bereaved believers reach across to the "other side" to contact their late loved ones. In 1908 Julia predicted that Stead would soon receive the money he needed to start the venture from America. She was right. Soon William Randolph Hearst hired Stead as a special correspondent. With the money he earned, Stead was able to open Julia's Bureau in 1909. (Chronically short of money, the bureau finally closed in 1912.)

Although his fascination with spiritualism continued throughout his life, Stead was equally committed to pacifism. Never afraid to take an unpopular stand, Stead was in direct opposition to the government of England, which was rallying support for the Boer War. In 1898, after visiting Tsar Nicholas of Russia,

Stead was inspired to found the weekly paper *War Against War*. He also led a peace crusade opposing the Boer War and published the weekly newspaper of the Stop the War Committee. Stead spent the rest of his life crusading for peace through arbitration.

Perhaps based on his premonition that "something good" was coming from his voyage on the *Titanic,* Stead was not afraid as the disaster began to unfold around him. When Steward Andrew Cunningham came to help Stead don his lifebelt, the old gentleman complained it was all "a lot of nonsense." As the *Titanic* slowly began to sink and passengers ran up onto the deck, scrambling to get into the lifeboats, Stead made no attempt to join the frantic masses. Instead, he simply retired to the First Class Smoking Room with a book.

It seems as if Stead may have gotten what he wanted from his voyage on the *Titanic.* Although his body perished, his spirit reportedly lingered behind. Stead appeared in his office three weeks later in front of his daughter, his secretary, and several other women according to *The Encyclopedia of Ghosts and Spirits* by Rosemary Ellen Guiley, who reports, "They claimed his face shone radiantly as he called out, 'All I told you is true!'"

April 15, 1912, 12:05 a.m.

After assessing the damage and conferring with Thomas Andrews, managing director of the shipyard that built the Titanic and a passenger on her maiden voyage, Captain Edward Smith can reach but one conclusion: The unsinkable ship is going down. He gives the order to uncover the lifeboats and rouse the passengers—knowing full well there are enough boats for only about half of those on board.

THE STARLET WHO PLAYED HERSELF

Dorothy Gibson

lthough many lost everything in the sinking of the *Titanic,* at least one First-Class passenger managed to use the disaster as a career stepping stone.

Dorothy Gibson of New York, New York, was a model striving to become an actress in the fledgling motion picture industry. In March of 1912 Gibson had just completed her first film, a one-reeler called "The Easter Bonnet." Ready for a rest, she sailed on March 17 with her mother, Pauline Gibson, for a brief European vacation. After enjoying the sights of Paris for just a few days, Dorothy was called back by her gentleman friend, wealthy New York film distributor Jules Brulatour.

The Gibsons were excited to be able book their return passage on the maiden voyage of the magnificent new *Titanic,* boarding when the ship docked at Cherbourg on the evening of April 10.

When disaster struck on April 14, Gibson and her mother were the first two passengers to enter lifeboat No. 7, the first boat launched from the *Titanic.* With them came the bridge partners with whom they had just passed a jolly evening, William Sloper and Fred Seward. As the Gibsons boarded the lifeboat, it seemed more like they were embarking on an adventure than fleeing disaster. Most of the *Titanic's* passengers were still not aware of the peril they were in, so there was no rush to leave the warm, well-lit ship for the icy blackness of the Atlantic. No. 7 sailed off with only 19 or 20 passengers, although it was built to hold up to 60. Later, when the adventure really had turned to disaster, water began gushing up through a hole in the bottom of No. 7. According to Dorothy Gibson, "This was remedied by volunteer contributions from the lingerie of the women and the garments of the men."

After her rescue by the *Carpathia,* Dorothy's new-found celebrity as a *Titanic* survivor gave her fledgling career the boost it needed—at least temporarily. On her return to the U.S., Dorothy acted in a silent one-reeler called "Saved From the *Titanic"* in which she played herself. Her costume for the production was the very dress she had worn the night the *Titanic* went down. Produced by the Eclair Moving Picture Company and directed by Etienne Arnaud, the film was released on May 14—

barely a month after the actual sinking. Although the real Dorothy Gibson was literally the first one off the *Titanic,* in the melodramatic film version of her story Dorothy is one of the last passengers to leave the sinking ship. No copies of the film are known to exist today.

Gibson made just one other movie, "Revenge of the Silk Masks," also in 1912. Two years later Gibson married Brulatour, but the marriage lasted just two years. She died in Paris of a heart attack in 1946.

April 15, 1912, 12:45 a.m.

Passengers in various states of dress and undress wander up to the deck, curious to find out what is going on. Without much sense of urgency, the crew begins loading women and children into the lifeboats. Many passengers are waiting to see what happens, still hoping everything will be righted soon so they can go back to bed instead of out into the black night. The first lifeboat, No. 7, lowers into the icy Atlantic. It is less than half full.

The Playboy Who
Went Down a Gentleman

Benjamin Guggenheim

s the unambitious son of one of the richest men in New
York, Benjamin Guggenheim was spoiled, arrogant, will-
ful—and determined to live life his own way. On the *Ti-
tanic*, faced with his own mortality and the supreme will of nature, he still
lived life his own way, choosing to face his fate like a gentleman.

Benjamin Guggenheim was the son of mining and smelting tycoon Meyer
Guggenheim, who had come to the United States penniless from Switzer-
land in 1848. Starting life in his new country as a door-to-door peddler,
Meyer began building his fortune by importing and selling Swiss lace. In
1881 he bought shares in two Leadville mines that proved to hold rich
stores of silver and lead. (The husband of fellow Titanic

passenger Margaret Tobin "Molly" Brown would strike it rich in another Leadville mine three years later.)

Most of Meyer Guggenheim's seven sons were well known for their phi-lanthropy. Daniel began a foundation to promote "the well-being of mankind," as well as the School of Aeronautics at New York University. Murry established a foundation that set up free dental clinics for the needy. Simon's foundation offered educational grants to deserving stu-dents. And Solomon founded the Guggenheim Museum in New York City, designed by Frank Lloyd Wright and housing a world-famous col-lection of paintings, sculpture and other works of art.

Sixth son Benjamin did not share his brothers' ambitions. When Benjamin Guggenheim boarded the Titanic in Cherbourg, he was 46 years old and Meyer had been dead for seven years. Instead of following his brothers' ex-ample and carrying on Meyer's name with good works, Benjamin was known for simply carrying on—with lavish living, much of it abroad, and bad investments on which he reputedly squandered some $8 million. Ben-jamin's wife, Florette, patiently waited at home while he cavorted with a se-ries of mistresses from one exotic locale to another.

Guggenheim's entourage on the Titanic included his valet, Victor Giglio, and his mistress of the moment, French singer Leontine Aubert. Guggenheim's chauffeur Rene Pernot was also on board, traveling in Second Class. As the *Titanic* began to sink, it fell to Bedroom Steward Henry Samuel

Etches to come to Guggenheim's cabin to help the passenger don his lifebelt. Ignoring Guggenheim's protests that "this will hurt," Etches finally managed to get the uncomfortable lifebelt onto the recalcitrant passenger. Etches then insisted Guggenheim put on a thick sweater and sent Guggenheim and Valet Giglio up to the boat deck with the rest of the First-Class passengers.

After looking around at the harried humanity on the boat deck, Guggenheim soon came back to his cabin, where he traded the sensible sweater for his finest evening wear. Giglio did likewise. Guggenheim was later heard to remark, "We've dressed up in our best and are prepared to go down like gentlemen."

In his last known act, Benjamin Guggenheim wrote a message which he handed to a woman as she boarded one of the lifeboats: "If anything should happen to me, tell my wife I've done my best in doing my duty."

When the rescue ship *Carpathia* pulled into New York Harbor, Guggenheim's wife and three of his nephews rushed to the dock. At the same moment, just out of Florette's earshot, an officer introduced an attractive young woman debarking the boat as "Mrs. Benjamin Guggenheim."

APRIL 15, 1912, 2:05 A.M.

As the last lifeboat pulls away into the night, a sort of calm settles over the Titanic. Captain Smith makes his way to the wireless shack where the operators are still on duty, trying vainly to make contact with other ships in the area. "Men, you have done your duty," the Captain says solemnly. "You can do no more. Abandon your cabin. Now it's every man for himself."

THE COUPLE DEATH
COULD NOT SEPARATE

Mr. and Mrs. Isidor Straus

T he best-remembered lovers on the *Titanic* were not a star-crossed young woman from First Class and a doomed young man from Third Class. They were a couple in their 60s who had shared a long, full life—and chose to stay together no matter what the future brought.

German-born Isidor and Ida Straus were returning home to New York after a pleasant winter vacation with their daughter. Married 41 years, the couple had earned their rest, having raised six children, built one of the nation's largest retail businesses, and distinguished themselves in both public service and philanthropy.

Isidor Straus was born in Rhenish, Bavaria, on February 6, 1845. When he was 9 the Straus family emigrated to the U.S., settling in Talbotton, Georgia, where Isidor's father Lazarus opened a dry goods business. By the time he was a teenager, Isidor was a clerk in his father's store. When the Straus family moved to Columbus, Georgia, at the start of the Civil War, 17-year-old Isidor found work as a blockade runner.

After the war, Isidor and his brother Nathan moved to New York and put their retail experience to work for R.H. Macy & Company. It was to be a defining moment. After 30 years helping to build the company into a national retail giant, Isidor took over ownership of Macy's in 1896.

At the age of 26, Straus had married 22-year-old Ida Blun. The two were inseparable from the start, writing each other every day when they were apart, using pet names for each other, and even celebrating their different birthdays on the same day.

Besides a full and happy family life and a talent for business, the Strauses also had a commitment to improving the world in which they and their children lived. Isidor represented New York as a Congressman from 1895 to 1897 and served on the boards of numerous financial and philanthropic institutions.

In early April of 1912 Isidor and Ida traveled to Europe on the German liner *Amerika*. The party also included their daughter Beatrice, Isidor's manservant John Farthing, and Ida's maid Ellen Bird. Two weeks later they booked their return passage on the *Titanic* (without Beatrice, who had decided to remain behind), boarding at Southampton.

When it became clear that the *Titanic* was going down, officers and friends —including Colonel Archibald Gracie, a member of the prominent New York family that built Gracie Mansion, the mayor's residence—insisted that Ida get into a lifeboat. She stepped into No. 8, the fifth boat to leave. But as soon as Isidor backed away, Ida hopped out, flatly refusing to leave her husband's side. No amount of persuasion could change her mind. "We have been living together for many years. Where you go, I go," she insisted. Ida handed her fur coat to Maid Ellen Bird saying, "I won't need this anymore." Bird got into the boat and was later rescued. Isidor and Ida Straus were last seen sitting quietly together on a pair of deck chairs.

Isidor's body was identified and buried at Beth-El Cemetery in Brooklyn. The family later had it moved to Woodlawn Cemetery in the Bronx where they had an elaborate mausoleum built. Ida's body was never recovered.

Andrew Carnegie eulogized the couple at a memorial service where they were fondly remembered by 6,000 mourners.

APRIL 15, 1912, 2:20 A.M.

From the lifeboats, passengers watch in horrified shock as the bow of the mighty Titanic sinks deeper and deeper into the water and her stern rises up into the air. Eventually the ship is almost perpendicular to the water—sending all who remain on the deck plunging downward into the icy Atlantic. Finally the Titanic breaks in two and slides beneath the water. All that remains is smoke and debris.

THE TWO WHO LOOKED
THE OTHER WAY

Sir Cosmo and Lady Lucille Duff-Gordon

"There is your beautiful nightdress gone!" It seemed a harmless observation, but it changed the lives of Sir Cosmo and Lady Lucille Duff-Gordon forever. Why? Because Lady Duff-Gordon made this wistful comment to her secretary from the relative comfort of mostly empty lifeboat No. 1—over the cries of more than 1,500 of her fellow *Titanic* passengers who were drowning in the sea around her. Not since Marie Antoinette offered to "let them eat cake" had a statement unintentionally stirred such ire—or provoked such controversy.

At 48, Lady Lucille Duff-Gordon, the former Lucille Wallace Sutherland, was a fashion designer with chic shops in London, Paris and New York. She had met her aristocratic 49-year-old husband when she was a designer with a fashion house of which he was on the board of directors. Childless, they had been married since 1900.

The Duff-Gordons had boarded the *Titanic* at Cherbourg along with Lady Duff Gordon's secretary, Laura Mabel Francatelli. As the *Titanic* began to sink, the three took their seats on lifeboat No. 1, which was lowered at 1:10 a.m. with only 12 people aboard—seven of them crew members. The boat was designed to hold as many as 60.

As the cries of those in the water grew increasingly desperate, fireman Charles Hendrickson suggested rowing back to see if they could help. Lady Duff-Gordon strenuously objected, arguing that the boat might be swamped and overturned. Several of the men agreed it would not be a good idea to turn back.

When Lady Duff-Gordon uttered her ill-timed comment about the night-dress, it was the final straw for two sailors in the lifeboat. They immediately took exception—complaining to Lady Duff-Gordon it was quite one thing for her to speak about fine clothes when they had lost everything, including their future paychecks. Lord Cosmo stepped in to smooth things over, promising to give the sailors £5 each to replace their belongings. (He later kept his promise when they were safe aboard the rescue ship *Carpathia*.)

Eventually Hendrickson took a suggestion from another passenger to head for a light they could see in the distance. So the 12 survivors turned their backs on the hundreds of souls dying in the water and rowed toward the light—which proved to be the ship *Carpathia*, which rescued them later in the morning.

The Duff-Gordons did not fare well in the court of public opinion as the story of the *Titanic* disaster spread. Gossip among their upper-crust London set had Sir Cosmo bribing the crew to row away from the scene of the disaster with no regard for the victims who were still in the water. The gossip became a legal matter when Sir Cosmo was called before a packed British inquest to defend himself against an accusation that he had bribed the crew members in the lifeboat to secure his rescue. Cosmo was cleared, but the Duff-Gordons' reputations—and lives—were never the same again.

The Duff-Gordons continued to be shunned by many of their former friends and eventually drifted apart, although they never divorced. Lady Duff-Gordon's shops continued to do well for awhile, but went bankrupt before her death in 1935 at the age of 71. Sir Cosmo died in 1931 at age 68.

APRIL 15, 1912, 3:30 A.M.

Just as the sun begins to peek over the horizon, the half-frozen lifeboat passengers finally see the sight they have been waiting for: the rescue ship Carpathia. Shouts of joy and relief fill the frigid morning air. The long night is finally over. And despite the cold, all hands begin to row as fast as they can.

THE MEN WHO
BORE RESPONSIBILITY

The Crew of the Titanic

There had to be someone to blame for the *Titanic* disaster. Public opinion demanded it. And there were several likely candidates.

The Captain: Edward J. Smith

With 40 years at sea, Captain Edward Smith was the White Star Line's leading captain. He had planned on retiring earlier, but because his popularity reflected so well on the line, management coaxed him to make his final trip the maiden voyage of the *Titanic*.

Captain Smith

On the evening of April 14, Smith had read wireless messages from other nearby ships warning him of ice in the *Titanic's* path. Even so, he maintained the *Titanic's* speed. (This was accepted procedure according to other Atlantic captains who were questioned during the investigation of the *Titanic* disaster.) Smith did fail to provide effective leadership in other ways, however. He never held a lifeboat drill or developed any plans for managing emergencies. Although he remained calm and stoic as the ship went down, he never organized the evacuation effort—so while many crew members worked to get passengers up to the boat deck, a few tried to keep Third-Class passengers from crossing First- and Second-Class territory. Others had no idea what to do.

Smith went down with the ship, although eyewitnesses differ on the details. According to one account, he calmly walked onto the bridge as the icy waters closed over it. Another witness reported Smith raising a pistol to his head and pulling the trigger. A third account had Smith swimming toward a lifeboat with a baby in his arms, handing the baby to a passenger, then disappearing beneath the waves.

The Builder: Thomas Andrews, Jr.

Thomas Andrews Jr., 39, managing director of the Harland and Wolff Shipyard, had overseen the design and construction of the *Titanic*. Andrews spent most of his time during the voyage making notes and  helping the crew work out minor problems as they be- *Thomas Andrews, Jr.* came acquainted with the new ship. When the *Titanic* struck ice, Andrews was in his cabin looking over blueprints and working on his notes. He was unaware of any problem until he received a message from Captain Smith requesting him to come to the bridge at once. Andrews and Smith inspected the rapidly flooding mail room and squash court. Back on the bridge Andrews told Smith that the damage was fatal. He expected the ship to go down within two hours.

As the *Titanic* slowly sank, Andrews wandered the decks, encouraging passengers to wear their lifebelts and get to the lifeboats. He was last seen standing near the painting in the First-Class Smoking Room, without a lifebelt, staring into space.

The Wireless Operator: Jack Phillips

On the evening she sank, the *Titanic* had received six separate wireless messages from nearby ships warning of ice ahead. Not all of these messages were relayed to Captain Smith. The wireless operator on duty, 24-year-old First Operator John George "Jack" Phillips (who celebrated his birthday on-board the *Titanic*) was actually an employee of the Marconi Wireless

Jack Phillips

Company. Ship-to-shore wireless transmission was still something of a novelty—more a convenience than an essential and official form of communication. The operators' main job was sending personal telegrams for paying customers—the passengers. Thus it was quite easy for Phillips to ignore the blitz of ice warnings he had received throughout the evening of the *Titanic's* sinking. They simply weren't his top priority. Phillips went down with the ship.

The Manager: J. Bruce Ismay

One found guilty in the court of public opinion was the managing director of the White Star Line. Belfast native J. Bruce Ismay, 50, had inherited the business from his father, Thomas, who had bought White Star when Bruce was five years old and subsequently built it into a fleet of great steamships providing quick, comfortable and reliable service between England and America.

J. Bruce Ismay

Thomas Ismay was a hard father and Bruce grew up defensive, cantankerous and arrogant—yet oddly shy. Three years after his father died in 1899, Bruce sold the White Star Line to J.P. Morgan, staying on with the company as manager. The shipping business was hotly competitive and Ismay was positioning White Star ships as perhaps not as fast as those of the rival Cunard Line, but larger and more luxurious. The *Titanic* was his crowning achievement.

Instead of working like Thomas Andrews, Ismay enjoyed the *Titanic's* maiden voyage like any other passenger. He was asleep when the *Titanic* struck the iceberg. At about 11:50 Ismay made his way to the bridge wearing an overcoat over his pajamas. After learning the seriousness of the damage from Captain Smith, Ismay went down to the boat deck where crewmen had begun to uncover the lifeboats, barking orders to them to load the passengers faster. By 1:40 what Ismay thought was the last remaining lifeboat, Collapsible C, had been loaded with with 27 women and children. (There was actually another boat remaining, Collapsible D.) The officer in charge called for more women, but none came forward. Ismay looked around. Not seeing any other passengers, and with the water steadily climbing up the bow, he climbed in.

Once safe on the Carpathia, Ismay learned more than 1,500 souls had gone down with the *Titanic*—about two-thirds of the passengers and crew including the captain, Thomas Andrews, luminaries like John Jacob Astor and Benjamin Guggenheim, and even Ismay's own butler and secretary. Nervous to the point of collapse, Ismay withdrew to the cabin of the ship's doctor, where he holed up for the rest of the voyage under heavy opiate sedation. The doctor said Ismay "kept repeating that he ought to have gone down with the ship."

Although officially acquitted of wrongdoing in the investigation of the disaster, Ismay was reviled by press and public. He retired from the White Star Line, continuing to serve on the boards of several other companies. Ismay never discussed the *Titanic* and died of a stroke in 1937 at the age of 75.

Were these men responsible? Yes. But at the same time, no one thing any one of them did caused the *Titanic* disaster. Ultimately, the cause was much larger than any man. It was a pervasive combination of arrogance, indifference, and complete trust in mankind's own cleverness. It was a Greek tragedy played out in the icy waters of the North Atlantic.

April 18, 1912, 9:35 a.m.

As some 40,000 family members, friends, curious bystanders and reporters stand in the rain watching from shore, the Carpathia slowly makes its way past the Statue of Liberty into New York Harbor. For the 704 survivors of the Titanic, the voyage is finally over. But for the other 1,503 Titanic passengers and crew members, there will be no homecoming—today or ever.

41

AFTERWORD

The impact of the Titanic disaster was swift and profound. Before the Cunard ship *Carpathia,* which picked up all the *Titanic* survivors, had even reached New York, the United States Senate had organized an investigating committee chaired by Republican William Alden Smith of Michigan. As the *Carpathia* docked in New York, Senator Smith personally marched onto the ship to summon J. Bruce Ismay to attend a hearing scheduled for the next day.

Hoards of reporters were also waiting for the *Carpathia.* Carr Van Anda, managing editor of the *New York Times,* made the biggest score, bringing along Gugliemo Marconi to secure an interview with the *Titanic's* surviving wireless operator, Harold Bride. Nearly a century later, Bride's moving description of the tragedy remains one of the definitive accounts:

> *From aft came the tunes of the band. It was a rag-time tune. I don't know what. Then there was 'Autumn.' Phillips* [the other wireless operator] *ran aft and that was the last I ever saw of him alive.*
>
> —New York Times, *Friday, April 19, 1912*

Meanwhile, the Senate committee unrelentingly questioned Ismay, demanding to know exactly what influence the managing director might have had on the ship and its navigation and dissecting his behavior throughout the voyage and the sinking. Smith also questioned surviving crew members and passengers about Ismay's conduct. It became clear that—officially, anyway—Ismay and the White Star Line could not be held directly responsible for the disaster or its aftermath. Ismay had not tried to influence Captain Smith to try for a speed record, he had not controlled the launching of the lifeboats, he had not prevented any other passenger or crew member from escaping. Moreover, the *Titanic* had more lifeboat capacity than the British Board of Trade required. In short, Ismay's failure was more moral than legal. His crime was surviving when so many others had died.

The Senate committee also pursued Marconi, employer of the wireless operators, to find out if some conspiracy with Ismay or other White Star officials had tried to keep the horrible news of the *Titanic's* sinking and the huge loss of life from the press and public. Again, there was no evidence of misconduct. But Senator Smith expressed moral outrage that Bride had sold his story to the *New York Times*.

In the end, the Senate committee blamed the *Titanic* disaster largely on "laxity of regulation" by the British Board of Trade and passed tighter shipping regulations and new controls on wireless communications. The new regulations were mostly for show: The *Titanic* disaster was a wake-up call that caused the shipping lines to institute their own reforms. All shipping lines immediately ordered enough lifeboats for every person on all their ships. The White Star Line refitted the *Titanic's* sister ship, the *Olympic*, to float with up to six watertight compartments flooded. The shipping lines also collaborated to voluntarily reroute their courses farther south during seasons when icebergs were a threat.

On the other side of the Atlantic, the British Board of Trade made its own investigation. Again, J. Bruce Ismay took the witness stand. Hadn't he suggested holding a speed trial sometime before the ship reached New York? Hadn't the captain shown him a wireless warning that the ship might encounter ice? Ismay claimed he "had nothing to do with the navigation." As to the lifeboats, Ismay denied any part in deciding how many the ship should carry. He admitted that when he stepped into his own lifeboat, he knew that there must still be passengers below who had not yet been evacuated. "I was really not thinking about it," he said. It was an embarrassing moment—for Ismay, for the White Star Line, and for everyone involved. But in the end, the investigation found that Ismay had no "moral duty…to wait on board until the vessel foundered." He was officially off the hook.

One man who did pay a quantifiable price was Captain Stanley Lord of the ship *Californian,* which was traveling near the *Titanic.* On April 14, the *Californian* encountered a field of ice and stopped for the night. In the distance, the crew spotted another ship firing rockets. The *Californ-ian's* wireless operator had gone to bed and Lord chose not to awaken him to try to find out what was wrong. The next morning Lord and the crew of the *Californian* discovered the *Titanic* had gone down. They sped out to the site of the wreck but arrived too late. Lord did not mention having seen the rockets in his log, hoping to avoid controversy, but two of the *Californian's* crewmen leaked the information to the American press. During the investigation Lord claimed the *Titanic* was not visible from the *Californian*—it must have been some other ship firing rockets. Of course, whether the ship was the *Titanic* or not, Lord still had an obligation to come to its aid. In the name of public relations, Lord was fired, and he has gone down in popular legend as one of the primary villains in the story of the *Titanic*.

Villains or heroes—they all act their roles in the drama of the *Titanic*, if not necessarily in the reality. Because although the story of the Titanic reads like fiction, real life is never so black and white. The story of the *Titanic* is about real men and women in life-and-death circumstances the rest of us can only begin to imagine. Some of these flesh and blood human beings rose to the occasion, fulfilling what we—their audience—believe was their moral obligation. Others did not.

It is this drama that holds our fascination after all these years. How would *we* have behaved as the water began to creep up the *Titanic's* deck? Would we have been like Molly Brown—fighting with the lifeboat captain to go back for those still stranded in the water? Or would we have been at the other end of the spectrum with the Duff-Gordons—so self-involved that we were oblivious to the cries of hundreds of people dying all around us? Perhaps we would have fallen somewhere in the middle of the moral spectrum: complacent and disbelieving until it was too late to act, like John Jacob Astor. Or determined to continue making our own decisions no matter what, like Benjamin Guggenheim.

To realize just how much the world changed after the *Titanic* disaster, consider the sinking of the liner *Andrea Doria* off the New England coast 44 years later. There was no *Titanic* orchestra, bravely switching from ragtime

to hymns as the waters closed over the ship. There were no stokers working in the belly of the ship until the water engulfed them. On the *Andrea
Doria,* some crewmen reportedly just headed straight for the lifeboats,
leaving terrified passengers behind to fend for themselves.

One thing is certain about the *Titanic*—both myth and fact. Its disastrous
end made us look into the mirror of our own society in ways we never
had before. When we did, we saw some scenes that uplifted us and
some that disgusted us. We also saw that our unconditional belief in
technology was gone. And never again were we able to remain quite so
blissfully oblivious to the icebergs that lay in our path. Never again were
we able to trust that our world was so unsinkable that the lifeboats were
just for show. We want the lifeboats.

Printed in Great Britain
by Amazon

74480531R00037